# A DOCTOR'S PRESCRIPTION FOR A LIFE OF JOY, LOVE, AND PEACE

## DR. JOSEPH H. RIDGIK

Halo
PUBLISHING
INTERNATIONAL

Copyright © 2018 Dr. Joseph H. Ridgik
All rights reserved.

No part of this book may be reproduced in any manner without the written consent of the publisher except for brief excerpts in critical reviews or articles.

ISBN: 978-1-61244-637-0
Library of Congress Control Number: 2018903005

Contact the author Dr. Joseph H. Ridgik
Email: mridgik@comcast.net

Printed in the United States of America

Halo Publishing International
1100 NW Loop 410
Suite 700 - 176
San Antonio, Texas 78213
Toll Free 1-877-705-9647
www.halopublishing.com
E-mail: contact@halopublishing.com

This book is dedicated to
my wife Mary Lou and our children:

Donna

Karen

Mark

Lisa

Denise

And our many grandchildren and great-grandchildren.

They are God's greatest gifts to me.

God had a great day
when he created women!!!

What went wrong before that???

Success is measured not by what
you own, but rather by what
you have made of yourself.

"Three may keep a secret,
if two of them are dead."
**-Benjamin Franklin**

"There are three faithful friends—
an old wife, an old dog
and some ready money."
**-Benjamin Franklin**

"God heals, and the
doctor takes the fee."
**-Benjamin Franklin**

"If a man could have half his wishes,
it would double his troubles."
**-Benjamin Franklin**

"A man wrapped up in himself
makes a small bundle."
**-Benjamin Franklin**

"True merit, like a river, the deeper it
runs, the less noise it makes."
**-Edward Wood
Fist Earl of Halifax**

"There was never a
good war, or a bad peace."
**-Benjamin Franklin**

"If you can talk with crowds
and keep your virtue,
Or walk with king—nor lose
the common touch,
If neither foes nor loving
friends can hurt you;
If all men count with you,
but none too much,

If you can fill the unforgiving minute
With sixty seconds' worth of distance run,
Yours is the Earth and everything that's in it,
And—what is more—
you'll be a man, my son!"
**-Rudyard Kipling**

"I shall past through this world but once.
Any good I can do, any good, therefore,
I can show to any human being,
let me do it now. Let me not defer
or neglect it, for I shall not
pass this way again."
**-Anonymous quotation on a card, as quoted in *A Memorial of a True Life: A Biography of Hugh McAllister Beaver* (1898) by Robert Elliott Speer**

Don't let anger consume you;
keep a gentle mind.

"If you have a chance to accomplish
something that will make things better
for people coming behind you, and

> you don't do that, you are wasting your time on this earth."
>
> **-Roberto Clemente, Hall of Fame baseball player**

Clemente died in the crash of a transport plane which was carrying food and medical supplies to a country in South America that had suffered great damage from an earthquake. He made the ultimate sacrifice in giving up his life for his fellow man.

> "Don't cry because it's over, smile because it happened."
>
> **-Dr. Seuss**

Give more than you planned to; give more of yourself, your time, your energy and your wealth. Your "extra" could make up for those who aren't giving enough. Remember, the Lord loves a cheerful giver.

> "When I was a boy of fourteen, my father was so ignorant, I could hardly stand to have the old man around. But when I got to be twenty-one, I was astonished at how much he had learned in seven years."
>
> **-Mark Twain**

# IF YOU LOSE, DON'T LOSE THE LESSON

No one goes through life undefeated.

Follow the R's
Respect for yourself—remember who you are and what your parents taught you.

Respect for others—respect them and their feelings, above all those with less than you. Treat others as you would like to be treated (that includes all of God's creatures).

Responsibility for all your actions—you did it, take the responsibility for what you did, and don't cast the blame on anyone else.

Remember that not getting what you want, might be the way it's supposed to be. God <u>does</u> listen to our prayers. And indeed, He grants our wishes, but in His time and in the manner that He knows is best for us.

# DON'T LET A MINOR DISPUTE RUIN A GREAT FRIENDSHIP

It can take a moment to say or do something to hurt a friend and destroy a long-standing friendship so choose your words wisely when speaking, and if you've hurt someone, apologize immediately. . . don't wait.

> "Great love and great achievements involve great risk."
> **-Author Unknown**

Both of the above require total resolve and dedication; loving someone or something may involve the risk of losing more than one might expect, but making such a commitment overcomes any risks taken. Looking at the deeds of the early explorers, battlefield heroes, scientists, and any individual who had a dream or belief that seemed too much to accept. . . the risks we think are so great, pale in comparison to those taken by others before and around us.

## QUIET TIME

Spend some quiet time alone every day.
Begin and end each day with your thoughts; in the morning, think of the day ahead and plan to make it useful and fulfilling. At the end of that day, close your eyes before falling asleep and ask yourself if you did your best. If the answer is no, then renew

your strength with a good night's rest and start all over in the morning.

## OPEN YOUR MIND TO CHANGE, BUT DON'T LET GO OF YOUR VALUES

"Be not the first by whom the new are tried, nor yet the last to lay the old aside."
**-Alexander Pope**

This is an old idea but very true in this matter; keep an open mind and weigh the options. "Going with the flow" could mean swimming upstream at times. If you think you're right, go with your conscience, and you can't go wrong.

## CONSIDER THINGS FROM ALL ANGLES

Life isn't always like a true or false test where there's only one answer or solution. It's really more like an essay test: reasons must accompany actions.

## BELIEVE IN YOURSELF

Inner strength is at the core of this idea. Be confident; there's a big difference between confidence and cockiness. The latter is almost always an indicator of false bravado, and it is often used to cover insecurities.

Non-believers are negative people. . . don't be like them. Is there any such thing as a good negative? Self-belief and self-esteem go hand in hand. Avoid negative people, things, and habits.

## LOVE YOURSELF AND OTHERS WILL TOO

This isn't about ego or vanity; this is about an inner love which acknowledges that God only made one person like me. . . He had to love me to do that, and therefore I should love myself.

## MAKE IT HAPPEN

Don't be afraid to make a decision. Be a leader and not someone who goes along with the pack. Remember, if you're not the lead horse, the view is always the same. (Think about that.)

## OPEN YOUR EYES AND SEE THINGS AS THEY REALLY ARE

Think of being narrow-minded as "squinting with your brain." If your eyes are closed, so will your mind be.

# WHO SAYS WE CAN'T LIVE IN THE PAST?

Live a good and honorable life so when you get older, you can look back and enjoy it again. Some of my greatest joys arise when my thoughts wander back to the "good old days" of my childhood: my family and my life in general. Some of my greatest pleasure comes when my grandchildren ask me what it was like "way back when". . . Ours was "the greatest generation," and we have a duty to tell our story of times when life was simple and a handshake was your sign of honor and integrity.

> "Silence is sometimes the best answer."
> **-Dalai Lama XIV**

Often, by not replying to a statement or question, it can imply that the subject might require much more thought than the person asking for the answer realized. Think before you answer. . . We all like to think that our opinion is valued, and while this can be a pleasant boost to our ego, remember that silence can mean "I don't know." There's nothing wrong or weak in saying that you don't have the answer.

# PRACTICE MAKES PERFECT

It's been said that nothing or no one is perfect, but why not strive for perfection? This requires a strong work ethic, both mentally and physically. Be the very best you can be.

Don't worry about growing old—that should concern you only if you haven't done the best throughout your life. One of the many rewards of old age is the comfort and peace of mind in knowing that you did the best you possibly could. There is no reward for having done nothing. Don't stand before God with an empty slate.

# WHETHER YOU CHOOSE TO BE OR NOT, YOU ARE A ROLE MODEL FOR YOUR CHILDREN AND GRANDCHILDREN

I worshipped my parents and grandparents, and even though my formal education was more extensive than theirs by far, early in my life I recognized the fact that they were much "smarter" than me. They lived through many times that were so much more difficult than you or I could ever imagine... They graduated from the famous "College of Hard Knocks." I can never remember being embarrassed by them, and I would never think of embarrassing them; I admired everything they represented: love, family, hard work, accountability, and devotion to God.

## KEEP YOUR SENSE OF HUMOR, BECAUSE JUST LIKE THE MIND, IT'S A TERRIBLE THING TO LOSE

Be able to laugh at yourself (above all as you get older). Start your day by reading the comics section of the newspaper. Don't let others drag you down. Be that individual that others want to be around.

## LEARN FROM YOUR MISTAKES; IF YOU MAKE ENOUGH OF THEM, YOU MIGHT END UP BEING BRILLIANT

Some people do virtually nothing with their lives because they're afraid of making a mistake. How else can we learn, if not by trial and error? The object is to not repeat the same mistakes and to correct the errors.

## WHAT'S TRULY VALUABLE SHOULDN'T BE HELD IN YOUR HAND BUT IN YOUR HEART

Worldly possessions are just that— worldly—but it's what we've done for others, and with our own lives, that matters most, and often our only measurement is what we know and feel in our hearts.

## IT'S BETTER TO WEAR OUT THAN TO RUST OUT

Keep moving mentally and physically. Treat your body as you would a unique car, a car without a reverse gear. Look at some individuals who, despite severe handicaps, led very productive lives. Read the biography of Helen Keller.

## GROWING OLD DOESN'T MEAN THAT YOU HAVE TO STOP GROWING

We grow in countless ways... in our love for our spouses, our family members, the world around us, and all the beauty in it. We grow in wisdom and experience, and we grow the seeds that we have planted in our own garden of life.

Some of the wealthiest and/or most educated people you meet may not have the least bit of common sense.

Have you ever seen a high school or college course in "common sense 101"? Common sense involves reasonable thinking and decision making.

## DON'T FORGET HOW TO PLAY

Some of the most wonderful words you'll ever hear (if you should be so fortunate), might be. . . "grampop or grammon, you're so silly." That's truly music to my ears. Get down on the floor and play with the little ones. It may take a few minutes to get on your feet again, but it will be well worth the trip.

## HAVE NO FEARS ABOUT GROWING OLD; ENJOY THE RIDE

Should you be fortunate enough to live a long life, be thankful and consider it a blessing. Think of what you've seen and done, rather than what was missed by those who didn't have the privilege of old age. Old age *is* a privilege.

## IT DOESN'T MATTER HOW LONG YOU WERE ON THE ROAD OF LIFE, BUT WHAT DOES MATTER IS HOW WELL IT WAS TRAVELED

Make your life a road well-traveled—make the most of it. Each of us is a living history book, and we pass that history on to those around us and to those who follow us.

## FRIENDS ARE LIFETIME GIFTS— CHERISH THEM ALWAYS

You can't make someone be your friend. Just as with precious, delicate flowers, friendships need nurturing and cultivation. Treat a friendship gently, value it, and nurture it.

> "Life is like riding a bicycle: you don't fall off unless you stop pedaling."
> **-Claude Pepper**

This is all about control and steering your life in the right direction. Pedaling, in this case, is walking, and whether we slip while walking or fall from the bike, all that matters is that we pick ourselves up, brush ourselves off, and move in the right direction: forward.

## DON'T CROSS BRIDGES BEFORE GETTING TO THEM

No one has ever succeeded in doing this, or even in crossing more than one bridge at a time. Simply face one problem at a time. Consider your brain to be a filter. . . a lot of raw material may enter it, and it is not until you have sifted through the debris that a single, pure product emerges.

## DON'T TAKE YOUR PROBLEMS TO BED WITH YOU

Someone may suggest that "you sleep on it," but that may not be the best advice because it could cause you to lose a night's sleep. Just close your eyes, take a deep breath, relax, and say a silent prayer. Ask for God's help. There's no better combination than a good, restful sleep and putting your worries in God's hands.

## BE A GOOD LISTENER

In listening, you hear ideas that are different from your own. It's hard to learn something new when you're doing all the talking. You will find that being a passive listener will get people to ask what your opinion is more often. There is an art to knowing when to shut up. Don't dominate the conversation.

## COUNT YOUR BLESSINGS

Be thankful for everything you have and every breath you take. We live in the best country on the planet and see and have more in one day than many people do in a lifetime. What's there to gripe about? Spread the news.

## PRAISE IS NICE, BUT AFFECTION IS THE GREATEST REWARD

Praise is a compliment. . . pleasant, but of little inner value. Affection implies love and love is deep and meaningful: something that is to be strived for. It's nice to have someone say you're a nice person, but wouldn't it be better if they said they loved you? I'd prefer the latter.

## BE THANKFUL FOR PLEASANT MEMORIES

If you're having a bad time, sit back, close your eyes, and reflect on some of the most pleasant times in your life. Your childhood is a good time and place to look back on, and those thoughts should be such that a smile will come to your face.

## DON'T BE AFRAID OF TOMORROW; YOU'VE ALREADY SEEN YESTERDAY, AND YOU'VE CONQUERED IT

Life can be full of challenges so take it slowly: day by day, one step at a time. Challenges and battles are won with strength and willpower. Look back on what you've already accomplished, and you may be pleasantly surprised by what you've done.

## IMAGINATION IS ONE OF THE MANY GIFTS GIVEN TO US—USE IT TO ITS FULLEST

Imagination isn't daydreaming; it's the mind's picture (image) of something that could exist. That image can be directed into reality. Consider the image as a blueprint that can be transformed into something real.

## DON'T EVER LET GO OF YOUR DREAMS

Some of the greatest accomplishments have come from the minds of dreamers. Keep your dreams in your heart and in your mind. What many may think unattainable, might be within easy reach for you.

## SELF-DISCIPLINE ISN'T THE SAME AS SELF-DENIAL

This means be committed to your plans and follow through; it does not mean inflexibility, but it does require hard work. George Bernard Shaw wrote: "I want to be thoroughly used up when I die, for the harder I work, the more I live."

## WHEN OPPORTUNITY KNOCKS AT YOUR DOOR, BE SURE TO OPEN IT

Seize the opportunity. If you sit around waiting for things to happen, they probably won't. Successful people don't wait for others to give them a break. They work for what they want, and they always work hard.

## SOME OF HISTORY'S GREATEST PEOPLE EXPERIENCED SOME OF LIFE'S GREATEST FAILURES

Read the biographies of Harry S. Truman, Abraham Lincoln, Thomas Edison, Mahatma Gandhi, and others. They overcame huge failures and were strengthened by these challenges. They more than persevered in the face of failure.

## BE HONEST

Almost always, any word that begins with "dis" suggests something negative: dishonesty, disloyalty, disbelief, and so on. Don't be dishonest. To <u>not</u> be honest is to be immoral. Don't have the attitude, "Everyone else is doing it." Set high moral standards and follow them. Honesty will give you peace of mind.

## THE SOUND OF LAUGHTER IS THE SWEETEST MUSIC

My worst days were brightened by the sound of my children's laughter and the smile on their faces, and that continues as I grow older. Now I am blessed with even more smiling faces, those of my grandchildren. Laughter is truly contagious, and if you're ever going to spread anything that's contagious, let it be laughter.

## FIND REASONS TO LAUGH AND BE JOYFUL

First, be able to laugh at yourself. We're all human and we all make mistakes, and when we're able to laugh at ourselves, we show others that yes, even if we mess up, it's not the end of the world. This will keep you humble in your heart and in the eyes of others.

## RARELY IS GOOD NEWS WRITTEN IN FINE PRINT

This goes along with the adage, "If it sounds too good to be true, it probably is." Be certain to read the fine print and don't be afraid to ask a lot of questions. There's no harm or shame in being skeptical when decision making is involved.

## GO ANYWHERE, AS LONG AS IT'S FORWARD

You can't change what happened yesterday so put that behind you. Today, as the saying goes, is the first day of the rest of your life, so move on. Nothing can be achieved by standing still or going in reverse. Other than when you're driving a car, you don't need a rear-view mirror.

## BEFORE STARTING A NEW SLATE, ERASE WHAT'S ALREADY THERE

Don't take on too heavy of a load. Don't spread yourself too thin. Did you complete what was planned or did you leave it half done? Try to do one thing at a time and do that well rather than attempt several things and do all of them poorly. Have you ever watched a juggler? It's a very chaotic scene, and even the best jugglers drop the ball at times. Life can be busy, which is good, but keep the chaos out of it.

## YESTERDAY CAN'T BE RELIVED; TOMORROW IS AN UNKNOWN; MAKE THE MOST OF TODAY

Live each day as if it's going to be your last. Wake up each morning with goals and a positive attitude and be certain to have some fun every day. Life is too short to waste a lot of time with negatives. A good today can make a great tomorrow.

## WRITE YOUR UNHAPPINESS IN DUST AND YOUR JOY IN MARBLE

Don't let bad things become deep scars in your mind. . . don't dwell on them. The longer you brood, the more deep-seated your unhappiness will become. Joy, like a swift, clear stream can wear away the hardest stone. Let your joy be a stream of happiness.

## LISTEN TO THE WISDOM OF THE ELDERLY

They have what we all hope to have someday and that is the wisdom of the ages. They have lived long and challenging lives. Your parents and grandparents have one of the most important gifts that takes years to achieve. . . EXPERIENCE. Talk to them at every opportunity, but more than anything, <u>listen</u> to them.

## INSTEAD OF BUILDING WALLS, BUILD BRIDGES

Don't isolate yourself. It's not pleasant being a loner. We're all members of one large family: the world. Reach out, join hands, and stay connected to your family and friends. Truly, as John Donne said, "No man is an island."

## KEEP YOUR MIND OPEN TO NEW IDEAS

This goes back to the idea of being a good listener, and in doing so new vistas will be opened to you. No matter how young or how old, the mind and the brain need to be exercised, and the best way to do so is to allow for room for new ideas. Don't be so self-centered as to think that only you can generate new ideas.

## TIME TRAVELS SLOWLY

To prove that time <u>does</u> travel slowly, quite often what you say to your children won't reach them until they're thirty or forty years old. One day you'll find yourself saying something that your mother or father said to you as a child. It's a frightening but true thought, but that's okay because they did a good job of raising you, didn't they?

## TRUST IN THE FUTURE— DON'T WORRY ABOUT THE PAST

Here's that word "worry" again. Don't dwell on yesterday. It's over and done with, and even if things didn't go as well as you would have liked, that can only make you stronger and more prepared for the future. You are the future, and so much of it is in your hands.

## WE CAN'T TURN BACK THE CLOCK, BUT WE CAN REWIND IT

Yes, what you've lived is behind you, and if you find yourself thinking there isn't anything left, you're in a rut. Take on new challenges. Try something you've always dreamed of doing. Take art or music lessons—anything—don't just sit there.

## SETBACKS ARE A PART OF LIFE; IT'S JUST HOW YOU HANDLE THEM THAT MATTERS

Who said life was going to be easy? Very few of us were born with a silver spoon in our mouths. Don't turn a setback into a retreat; setbacks imply a temporary event. The only footsteps in the sand you should want to see are the ones behind you.

## STRIVE TO LEARN SOMETHING NEW EVERY DAY

Each day should be a learning experience. Learn a new word and look up the definition in the dictionary. Read the newspapers and find the location of countries you read on a globe or in an atlas. Be inquisitive; don't ever stop asking questions. An often-repeated comment of yours should be, "I didn't know that."

## YOUNG OR OLD, DON'T USE AGE AS AN EXCUSE

As you grow older, make your age an advantage. With age comes maturity, experience, and wisdom. Grow old gracefully. I love looking into the eyes of the elderly. . . the sparkle says so much without even uttering a word.

## NEVER DOUBT THE POWER OF LOVE

Probably no word in the world has been written, sung, and talked about more than this one word. The opposite of love is hate, but love can overcome anything and everything, especially hate. Love is warm, tender, and not pretentious. It can melt the coldest, hardest heart.

## IF YOU'RE WRONG, HAVE THE COURAGE TO ADMIT IT AND TO SAY "I'M SORRY"

No one likes to admit that they're wrong and even less, to apologize. To be proven wrong (when you know you were wrong) is difficult and will put you in an awkward position. Why allow yourself to be placed in that situation? Be honest; it's so easy.

## STOP TRYING TO CONTROL YOUR LIFE; PUT IT IN GOD'S HANDS

Remember, everything we have comes from God. Take the gifts that you are given and use them to the fullest. Let God be your co-pilot; in fact, why not let Him do all the driving? You'll never get lost during the travels of the journey of life if you keep that in mind.

> "In his heart a man plans his course, but the LORD determines his steps."
> **-Proverbs 16:9 (NIV)**

## BE AN INSTRUMENT OF PEACE

This is from the prayer of St. Francis, and it should be a daily thought upon arising in the morning or before going to sleep at night. You <u>can</u> make a difference in the world just by the way you lead your life. No matter what religious belief you follow, get a copy of St. Francis. It takes less than a minute to read the prayer, but it can set standards that will last a lifetime.

> "Happiness is simple: supper, a soaring kite, jumping into a pile of leaves."
> **-John Burgess, writing about Charles Schultz (creator of "Peanuts")**

When I was growing up, we didn't have computers or video games, and very early in my life, we didn't even have a phone or a television! Sounds horrible, doesn't it? On the contrary, those were the greatest days of my life; we had a family that communicated, a family that ate dinner together each evening. Believe it or not, we actually sat by a radio and used our imaginations as we visualized what was going on as we listened. We didn't have e-mail; we wrote letters and learned how to express ourselves. Life was so simple, yet so beautiful. Talk to your parents and, above all, your grandparents about the "good old days." One of my greatest regrets is that my children or grandchildren were never able to experience my childhood.

## DON'T TOLERATE EVIL OR PEOPLE WHO DO EVIL THINGS

"All that is necessary for evil to triumph is for good men to do nothing." This is a quote by the 18th-century parliamentarian by the name of Edmund Burke. What he said then holds true now as much as it did almost three hundred years ago. Get involved, take a stand, and be counted in the name of justice. Help the poor and the downtrodden. In other words, help the little guy.

## NEVER GET TOO OLD TO STAND AND BE COUNTED

This applies to everything from the privilege of voting to what you feel to be the social or moral problems in society. Don't rely on others to do the job; you may be the one who must lead the charge, even though you didn't ask for a leadership role.

## YOU'RE ONLY YOUNG ONCE, BUT DON'T FORGET TO GROW UP

Remain young at heart, but allow yourself to mature as you grow older. You can have the combination of youthful exuberance and maturity, but don't try to act anything but your age.

## KNOW THE DIFFERENCE BETWEEN GROWING OLD AND GROWING OLDER

Some people never grow up. Growing up should be both physical and mental. Don't ever embarrass yourself by not acting your age, no matter how young or old you are.

## REMAIN TRUE TO YOUR VALUES

You were raised by your parents to be honest and productive. Don't let success change your values—it should only make them stronger. If success comes as a result of deception or dishonesty, then you've compromised your standards. Remember to do periodic morality checks.

## IF YOU GET SOMETHING FOR NOTHING, DON'T COMPLAIN ABOUT THE LACK OF QUALITY

Hard work almost always produces a quality product, and all good quality things last for a long time. The greater the effort, the greater the appreciation of the end product. Rewards are rarely given for non-effort. It's true—the more you put into something, the more you get out of it.

## DON'T EVER DOUBT GOD'S PRESENCE IN YOUR LIFE

Any doubts or questions? Just look around and see God's creation. Begin with the thought that you were born into a wonderful and loving family, and you live in one of the greatest countries in the history of the world. Your parents conceived you, but God created you. Think about it.

## UNCONDITIONAL ACCEPTANCE IS THE GREATEST TREASURE OF FRIENDSHIP

Take me as I am, warts and all. I know I'm not perfect, but I'm trying. This is not only true in friendships, but also in marriage, where loving couples are best friends. There is unconditional love and acceptance, with no strings attached.

## WARM AIR AND BRIGHT SUNSHINE ARE THE BEST MEDICINES FOR DEPRESSION

If you're feeling down, go to the beach, take off your shoes and socks, and walk along the shore. There's no better therapy than "hydro" therapy: the sound of the waves crashing into the sand.

## FORGIVENESS IS GIVEN TO YOURSELF AS MUCH AS TO OTHERS

To not forgive is to carry a grudge or to be hateful. If you've messed up, forgive yourself and move on, but do the same for others. We're all human and mistakes, big and small, happen.

## BE THE KIND OF FRIEND YOU WOULD LIKE TO HAVE

> "Do unto others as you would have them do unto you."
> **-Luke 6:31 (NIV)**

There is no better way to phrase it. This is a wonderful motto by which to lead your life. Treat others the way you'd like to be treated.

> "There are none so blind as those who will not see."
> **-English Proverb**

There are many ways to look at this; don't be narrow-minded. Consider other people's point of view. Not "seeing" can be the result of not agreeing or just plain stubbornness. You may have to close your eyes and see with your heart to get the proper perspective.

## OPEN YOUR EYES TO THE JOYS OF LIFE

Your eyes, mind, and heart should be like a wide-angle lens on a camera, taking in the scenes of daily life and what's around you. I love the term "bright-eyed and bushy-tailed." Simply put, it means being eager and excited about even the smallest things. Live your life in eager anticipation.

## EVERY DAY IS A NEW BEGINNING

That's the wonderful thing about this life of ours; you can forget about yesterday (you can't change it anyway) and start fresh. Remember what's been said so often: "Today is the first day of the rest of your life." Pick up your head and move on.

## LIFE CAN BE BEAUTIFUL; DON'T MISS IT

What's the alternative to living? So many clichés can be used to expand on this thought, but one of the best might be, "We go around only once in this world," so make the best of it and enjoy the ride.

## IF YOU FEEL THE NEED TO HAVE THE LAST WORD IN AN ARGUMENT, YOU SHOULD SAY, "I'M SORRY" OR "I APOLOGIZE"

You'll feel so much better if you end things this way and so much stronger for it. Ending an argument without an apology is like leaving an open wound; it will take a long time to heal.

## SERVE OTHERS AND YOU ARE SERVING GOD

This is why we were put on this earth: to help our fellow man. This life isn't about "me" or self-service. Remember, give and you shall receive. No one can measure the rewards of giving. How can you measure happiness?

> "By failing to prepare,
> you are preparing to fail."
> **-Benjamin Franklin**

Don't walk blindly into the situations you encounter during your life; get and stay organized. If you've ever been unprepared for an exam, that is how your life can be. . . chaotic and confused. Life is tough enough, but you can make it much simpler by planning ahead and not rushing into anything.

## DON'T WORRY ABOUT DYING; WORRY ABOUT NOT HAVING LIVED

It's true that no one leaves this world alive, so why not leave it with your mark firmly stamped on it? Be certain that your obituary is one that will make for an interesting read. On the subject of obituaries, make a habit of reading them, and not only those of notable people. Some "common" people have done many uncommon things.

## MAKE A DIFFERENCE IN SOMEONE'S LIFE

Help someone. Be a mentor, a Big Brother or a Big Sister. Just by your actions and examples, you can be a guiding light to someone less fortunate than you. There's no doubt that if you do good for someone, that person in turn will do the same for others. Be the center of the ripple effect.

## DON'T COMPLAIN ABOUT THE WEATHER— YOU CAN'T CHANGE IT

However, life, unlike the weather, can be changed. Take charge of your destiny. If you're not happy with your job, change jobs. There's nothing more frustrating than waking up each morning and dreading the thought of going to your workplace. Look for positive changes.

## LET GO OF UNPLEASANT THOUGHTS AND MEMORIES

Consider negative thoughts and memories as "acne of the mind." Get rid of the blemishes any way you can, and in doing that, permanent scarring will be prevented.

## ALWAYS TRY TO GO BEYOND WHAT YOU THINK ARE YOUR LIMITS

The greatest satisfaction comes from having climbed the mountain, i.e. having achieved a goal. The more difficult the climb, the greater sense of elation there is. When looking back, you may think: it wasn't difficult after all. Next time, set the bar even higher.

## LIFE IS LIKE A PENCIL—IF YOU DON'T GET THE LEAD OUT, YOU WON'T LEAVE A MARK

If a pencil breaks or the lead runs out, nothing happens... nothing shows up on the paper. Your goal should be to leave a mark and that mark should be bright-eyed and bushy-tailed.

## NO ACT OF KINDNESS IS TOO SMALL OR UNIMPORTANT IF IT BRINGS LIGHT TO SOMEONE'S DAY

"Reach out and touch someone." Does this sound familiar? Reaching out requires little or no effort; just smile or make a telephone call. These little touches can brighten the darkest day of a lonely or sad person. Be that bright light.

## LIVE YOUR LIFE WITH TRUE PURPOSE

Don't stagger through life. Get a grip early on about what you want to do and then do it. Don't look back someday and have any doubts about whether you could have done more or better. It might be too late at that time.

## DON'T WASTE A MOMENT OF ANY DAY IN SELF-PITY

Quit feeling sorry for yourself. Does it serve any purpose? Is there any benefit to it? Channel that pity into a challenge; whatever had me down, can't and won't keep me down. Move on.

## BE PATIENT WITH OTHERS, BUT ABOVE ALL WITH YOURSELF

Patience is a virtue. Patience doesn't imply delay or inertia; it means taking the time with others and yourself to pull back and evaluate the situation. Don't be a bull in a china shop and go charging in. Like the road sign says, proceed with caution.

# GET INTERESTED IN THE FUTURE—THAT'S WHERE YOU'LL BE SPENDING ALL YOUR TIME

This means getting involved and planning how you will impact the future. Not everyone can change the world but we can all have a positive effect on our own little world and those around us. Where do you want to be and <u>what</u> do you want to be?

# LET LOVING BE YOUR REASON FOR LIVING

Don't be afraid to say "I love you," and mean it! There's so much in our world and in our lives to love. To love means to enjoy, and life can be so enjoyable if you fill it with love.

> "No evil can happen to a good man, either in life or after death."
> **-Plato**

The two opposites in this statement—good and evil—can never exist in the same person. Read the lives of the Saints and see what evil good men suffered for God and their fellow man. We all have our own crosses to bear at times; know that rewards will come in one form or another, whether in this life or the next.

> "Even if you fall on your face,
> you're still moving forward."
> **-Victor Kiam**

I like this thought because it's about still plugging away even if things don't go as planned. There will be a lot of bumps in the road of life; don't let the bump become a hurdle that you can't overcome.

## ANYTHING OF WORTH CARRIES A MEASURE OF PAIN

This is all about sticking to your commitments and knowing that many times completing them can involve stress and anxiety; this pain is not necessarily of a physical nature. If something happens too easily, it may not have been worth doing.

## DESTROY YOUR ENEMIES BY MAKING THEM YOUR FRIENDS

This is paraphrasing a statement by Abraham Lincoln, and it is a testament to the power of love... love thine enemies. This can be one of the most difficult things to do and a tremendous challenge in life. This means turning the other cheek and accepting the fact that there are nasty people in this world, but maybe trying to reason with them and understand them can create a change in them.

> "It's better to keep your mouth shut and appear stupid than open it and remove all doubt."
> **-Mark Twain**

I love Mark Twain. He had simple but very practical ideas on how to live a good life. This particular quote essentially tells us not to get too full of ourselves. As we've said before, listening can make you a much better and more intelligent person, and in listening, the learning process continues.

## GRANDPARENTS DON'T HAVE TO DO ANYTHING BUT BE THERE

Oh, how I hope this is true because I've tried to do just that. Even though we were separated by many miles, grammom and grampop always communicated by mail and phone and let it be known that we were always available for our grandchildren. The greatest love in our lives is what we feel for our grandchildren and our great-grandchildren.

## SUCCESS IS MEASURED BY GOALS ACHIEVED, NOT ATTEMPTED

This is a good thought. This basically means that it's better to do one thing very well, the best you can, rather than get involved in several things and complete none of them or do them poorly. Don't leave things half done: that's like being half right.

## BE NICE TO NERDS; SOMEDAY THAT NERD MAY BE YOUR BOSS

Simply put, be nice to the little guy. Don't ever make fun of or pick on someone because they're different. Always remember: we're all God's children, and if you make fun of another person you're making fun of something God created. It's a guarantee that if you treat someone nicely, you'll feel as good as the person you befriended.

## CHOOSE YOUR WORDS CAREFULLY, YOU MAY HAVE TO LIVE WITH THE CONSEQUENCES OF WHAT YOU SAY

This applies not only to what you say but <u>how</u> you say it. Words said in anger are almost always spontaneous, which means they are spoken without thinking. Hurtful, thoughtless words can come back to haunt you. Try to put yourself on the receiving end of what you've said; in other words, how would I feel if someone said that to me?

## BRING OUT THE BEST IN OTHERS

Faulting others will do nothing but distance them from you. No one becomes successful by being a "loner." Successful people build strong relationships; listen to the ideas and opinions of others.

A tombstone always shows a person's date of birth and date of death; the dates are always separated by a line. "The line" tells the story of that person's life. The numbers (dates) mean nothing. The only thing that matters is what the line represents: what was done in those years. Just as with sports, when you step on the field (in this case the field of life) it's what you do between the lines that matters.

## IF YOU AREN'T INTERESTED IN THE BIGGEST PRIZE, THEN WHY EVEN COMPETE?

Face it—life can be a war with skirmishes and battles. Win most of the battles and you'll probably win the war. Competition never hurt anyone. It can only make you stronger.

## KEEP YOUR WORDS SOFT AND SWEET IN CASE YOU HAVE TO EAT THEM

Again, be careful of what you say and how you say it. A person can be as offended by the tone of your voice when you say something as he or she can be by what you say. It's so nice to be nice.

## FAILURE CAN BE A STIMULUS FOR SUCCESS

Try and try again. Learn from your mistakes and don't let the "F" word be part of your vocabulary. If something happens too easily, it may not be worth doing.

## DON'T WORRY

Worry is the least productive of all human activities. Above all, don't worry about things over which you have no control. Leave worrying to others, and say to yourself, "My mind can be put to better use than cluttering it up with something as negative as worrying."

## TAKE CHARGE OF YOUR LIFE

Start charting your life's course early. Make a list of your goals and dreams and make a point to review the list every year. Some things may change over the years, but you'll be amazed at how many of your dreams you will realize. Some of the most powerful people in America have done this, and they even continued to do so after having reached what they felt was the pinnacle of their careers.

> "Happiness lies in the joy of achievement and the thrill of creative effort."
> **-Franklin D. Roosevelt**

Effort and achievement are linked; the amount of effort that is invested often produces an achievement of equal worth. Great efforts equal great achievements, and it doesn't take much thinking to realize what minimal effort brings forth: not much.

## AS YOU MOVE ON IN LIFE, REMEMBER, IT'S NOT HOW OLD YOU ARE, BUT HOW YOU ARE OLD

I've known people in their eighties who were more fun to be around than someone who was thirty or forty years younger. Don't grow old before your time. Be fun to be around. Surround yourself with happy people and keep a positive attitude with positive thoughts.

## DON'T EVER STOP LEARNING

Learn something new every day. Read, read, read, and read some more. Read newspapers, magazines, and anything you can get your hands on. Learn a second language or a musical instrument; don't waste your mind. Your brain is like a muscle, and if it is not used regularly it will atrophy. (If you don't know what this word means, look it up, and you'll have learned something new today.)

## DON'T BARGAIN WITH GOD

God isn't a used car salesman. People tend to pray only if they need something or if they're in trouble.

Don't be the one who says, "God, I'll do this or that if you do this for me." It doesn't work that way. Good things come to those who pray daily. Let God get to know you.

## THE WORLD WILL ALWAYS NEED LEADERS: BE ONE

Not everyone can become president. Be a leader in your community, your family, and your church. One of the greatest forms of leadership is to lead by example. People follow strong leaders. It's true that some people are born leaders, but others grow into leadership roles. You might be one or the other.

## DON'T WORRY ABOUT SUCCEEDING; WORRY ABOUT FAILING

If you spend too much time worrying about failing, you won't have time to succeed. You might be concerned about the possibility of failure, but as Alfred E. Newman says, "What, me? Worry?" Direct your concern to everything good you're capable of doing.

## AGING ISN'T DECAYING

You've heard it before: it's better to wear out than to rust out. Aging is a form of growth in every sense, and some of the most beautiful creations in the world are its oldest, including people. Always respect the elderly; they have the wisdom of the ages, a wisdom you can hope to attain someday.

## RECOGNIZE YOUR TALENTS AND USE THEM WISELY

We all have talents; some people call them gifts. No matter what, they usually show themselves early in our lives. They may be subtle or obvious, but they're out there to be discovered. Gifts are to be used, enjoyed, and shared.

## IT'S NOT HOW LONG OR HOW HARD YOU WORK, BUT THE QUALITY OF WHAT YOU PRODUCE

Quality, not quantity is what we're talking about. Be efficient with time and energy; make every hour of every day count. Don't waste a moment. There's no greater sin than waste; make yours a life well-lived.

## DON'T MAKE EXCUSES IF YOU HAPPEN TO FAIL

Be honest with others and yourself. Remember, "To thine own self be true" (Shakespeare).

Admit it if you messed up. Others probably will recognize the fact that you goofed up so why wait for them to bring it to light? Respect will follow if you admit to your mistake. It takes a lot of effort and a guilty conscience to cover up, and mistakes will always show up.

## THERE IS DIGNITY IN BEING HONEST

Why even think of being dishonest? Dishonesty is lying, no matter how it's shaded. Sooner or later, liars get caught. Be straightforward in everything you do and everyone you deal with. Why are many politicians disliked? Because they make promises they rarely keep. Don't play politics with your reputation.

## SUCCESS WITHOUT HONOR IS UNACCEPTABLE

Listen to your conscience. It won't allow you to climb the ladder of success by stepping on or over people. There's a saying: "The devil made me do it," but that isn't so; individuals give in to the devil. He can't make you do anything unless you surrender to him. If you think you hear Satan knocking at your door, simply say, "God, could You answer that for me?"

## AT BEST, OUR NAMES ARE WRITTEN IN THE SAND, AND SOONER OR LATER THE SEA REACHES THEM AND ERASES THEM

William Saroyan once said, "Everybody has got to die, but I always believed an exception would be made in my case." Not so. There are no exceptions. But instead of the soft sand, etch your name and your deeds onto the hearts of those you meet along the way.

> "Man's reach should exceed his grasp."
> **-Robert Browning**

Basically, this means that a person should always be striving to do better. Take on the bigger challenges, and even though every you may not reach every goal, you can reach many of them. The object is to keep moving forward and to have many more plusses than minuses.

> "They are not dead who live in
> lives they leave behind."
> **-Hugh Robert Orr**

You may not leave a huge estate to your heirs, but you can leave a legacy of love and beautiful memories. Those left behind will forever want to imitate your life and that, in turn, will be passed on to their heirs.

## IT'S OKAY TO CRY

Grief is relieved by shedding tears that literally wash away the sorrow that we encounter along the way. Don't stifle the tears; it may appear that you've smothered the sadness, but it might be best to have a good cry. A feeling of relief follows.

## DON'T EVER FORGET TO KISS YOUR CHILDREN GOODNIGHT

A little kiss, a hug, and an "I love you" is the greatest security blanket a child can ask for. Stand by their beds and watch them as they sleep. The security goes both ways; you'll feel secure in knowing that they love you and that you are a wonderful parent.

## BE KIND TO ANIMALS

Feed a stray animal. They're God's creatures too. And while you're at it, take care of His human creatures also. Feed the poor and get involved in charitable work. Share your good fortune with the less fortunate, but be a "quiet" giver.

> "Hugs are one of the reasons
> we were given arms."
> **-Unknown**

What a simple gesture a hug is. What a silent statement it can make; it can express love, happiness, compassion, thanks. . . without ever saying a word.

> "I believe that [...] the world owes no man a living, but that it owes every man an opportunity to make a living.
> **-John D. Rockefeller**

The keyword here is opportunity. We all get opportunities at one time or another, and it's up to us not only to recognize them but to act on them. This is the greatest country in the world, with people coming from everywhere to seek its benefits. You already live here: go for it.

## MARRIAGES DON'T FAIL; PEOPLE IN MARRIAGES FAIL

Marriage is an enormous commitment and a lot of work; it is the ultimate form of teamwork. Marriages fail because it's too easy to get out of them. Couples marry with the idea that if it doesn't work out, they can go their separate ways, but that's a cop-out. Always look for your partner's good and nice qualities and don't dwell on their faults.

## RESPECT AGE

If something or someone is old, it was meant to be; old people, old customs, and old styles survive because they are fit to live and they are strong and they are unique in that quality. Respect age.

## QUALITY IS A GUARANTEE FOR CONTINUITY

What survives the test of time? Great books, great architecture, and paintings of the masters. Make your list. Be a quality person, lead a quality life, and your legacy will be bountiful.

> "A man is not finished when he is defeated. He is finished when he quits."
> **-Richard M. Nixon**

As long as you give your best effort, in your heart you know you can never lose. If you quit, you've not only lost at what you were doing, but you've lost self-esteem, self-confidence, and inner strength.

## IT'S BETTER TO BE ONE HOUR EARLY THAN ONE MINUTE LATE

Don't be a procrastinator. Get organized and have order in your life. Plan your day as you would your life. Living on the edge might be exciting for some activities but not in everyday living. Wake up each morning with a game plan. Make lists if necessary.

> "Laugh and the world laughs with you; Weep and you weep alone."
> **-Ella Wheeler, "Solitude" (1883)**

How true. This is an odd saying, but it reveals a lot. Essentially it's all about keeping a happy face. We all have times in our lives when we are down, but as quickly as you can, put these times behind you. A good sense of humor will take you a long way. Life's journey is tough enough as it is so why make it more unpleasant by having a negative attitude?

## KNOW AND BELIEVE THERE IS A GOD YOU CAN TALK TO

Atheists say there is no God, but their feelings may change as they near death. It's been said, "There are no atheists in a foxhole" and I truly believe that. As far as "talking" to God, this is simply taking quiet time and putting your life in God's hands, always thanking Him for all you have, and asking that He continue to watch over you.

> "One cannot stare at tragedy too long.
> It, like the sun, forces us to turn away."
> **-Fay Vincent, baseball commissioner from 1989-92**

This is a beautiful sentiment. Ella Fitzgerald said, "Into each life some rain must fall," and that means everyone, at one time or another, will be faced with difficulties, major or minor, some of a tragic dimension, but sooner or later we have to turn away from that setback and move on with our lives. We can't allow ourselves to be blinded by tragedy.

## LIFE'S RACE MAY BE LONG OR SHORT, BUT THE RACE IS ALWAYS WITH YOURSELF

Set a steady pace throughout your life. Don't burn out. Save your strength for the later part of your life.

## ALWAYS REMEMBER: GOD MADE ONLY ONE OF YOU. YOU ARE UNIQUE

You're an original—one of a kind—don't ever forget that. You are a creation of your parents' love. Don't ever diminish yourself.

## TO OVERCOME THE LOSS OF A LOVED ONE, CELEBRATE THE LIFE THEY LIVED

The death of my father, who died twenty years before my mother, was devastating, and for a time I was very angry at God. I soon realized that my father was a "loan" from God and that this "loan" was responsible for lifelong benefits I enjoyed. He was the standard by which I learned to live my life. He was a simple, hard-working man who loved life, family, and church, and he knew how to have fun. Whether he knew it or not, he celebrated life every day, and with his death, that celebration was carried on by all of us who knew and loved him.

> "We tend to live too far within self-imposed boundaries."
> **-William James**

This means that we limit our own abilities to act, and very often it is because of our own insecurities and perceived inadequacies. You can't ever know what you're capable of doing unless you test those capabilities and push them to the limits.

## ENJOY THE POWER AND BEAUTY OF YOUR YOUTH

It's been said that "youth is wasted on the young," and there is so much truth in that statement. To truly learn how to live and enjoy your youth, talk to the elderly, especially those who are vibrant and show no signs of slowing down. They are the best examples of how to go through life; take their experiences and try to incorporate them into your life, but do it while you're young.

## DON'T WASTE YOUR TIME ON JEALOUSY

If you find yourself envying someone else, it might be that you're really envious of their accomplishments, which in turn diminishes how you feel about yourself. Evaluate the reasons for your jealousy with the help of a trusted friend who can act as an unbiased arbiter.

## BE CAREFUL WHOSE ADVICE YOU ACCEPT

Use common sense, your "gut" instincts, and you'll seldom be wrong. The more advice you solicit, the more confused you'll be.

## LIFE'S TRUE JOYS ARE IN THE JOURNEY

One of the nicest things about a voyage is looking back at it. We can reflect on the "snapshots" in our memory album. I did my best and I enjoyed life.

## REGRET AND FEAR ARE TWIN THIEVES THAT CAN ROB US OF TODAY

Don't live a life of regrets; instead of saying "I'm sorry I didn't do this or that," just do it! When it comes to fear, the challenge is to overcome it, which can become one of life's great joys.

## CLIMB MORE MOUNTAINS; WALK BAREFOOT ON THE BEACH; WATCH MORE SUNSETS; LAUGH MORE; CRY LESS

There is not much more to be said; loosen up, relax, and don't take life too seriously.

> "The best way to cheer yourself up is to cheer somebody else up."
> **-Mark Twain**

This comes down to the joy of giving; give a smile, a hug, a handshake. Above all, give some time to others who need it.

## BRUSHING YOUR CHILD'S HAIR CAN BE ONE OF LIFE'S GREAT PLEASURES

If you enjoyed this little pleasure, return the favor and brush your child's hair; this simple act can bring both of you much closer.

## KNOW, LOVE, AND UNDERSTAND YOUR PARENTS; APPRECIATE THEM WHILE THEY'RE WITH YOU

Parents <u>do</u> try to do what's best for you. Be a good child and you'll be amazed at how nice your parents can be. You'll never know how much you'll miss them until they're gone. Tell them you love them. . . often.

If you try to understand your mother and father while you're young, that understanding will translate into the time when you become a parent.

Try putting yourself in your parents' shoes. Don't think it's easy being a parent. You may not want to hear this, but you'll never go wrong by raising <u>your</u> children the way you were raised.

If someone says something unkind about you, live your life so that no one will believe what they said.

The tongue can be sharper than the knife. Unkind people, people who disparage others, always get caught in their lies. Don't sink to their level. Be yourself and don't ever change your standards.

## THERE ARE PEOPLE WHO LOVE YOU DEARLY BUT JUST DON'T KNOW HOW TO SAY IT OR SHOW IT

Can you believe this could even be true of your sister or brother? As strange as it seems, know they'll be there for you in a pinch. Count on it.

## GRANDCHILDREN AND GRANDPARENTS ARE NATURAL ALLIES

Grandparents are a buffer or neutral zone between children and their parents; don't put your grandparents in the position of being arbiters or "go-betweens." Love and enjoy both your parents and grandparents as much as they love you.

Whenever you decide something with kindness, it will almost always be the right decision.

Again, think before you act. Ask yourself—how will my decision affect those around me, those I love?

## DON'T GIVE UP OR GIVE IN

Retreat and re-group but don't surrender. The greatest leaders had setbacks at one time or another, but they persisted because they had faith in themselves.

## GIVE MORE THAN YOU PLANNED TO

This doesn't only pertain to monetary giving. Reverse the saying, "Give 'til it hurts" and make it, "Give 'til it feels good."

## DON'T JUST BE GOOD; BE GOOD FOR SOMETHING

I hate the phrase "good for nothing." How can someone be good for nothing? Even if you're only good at one thing, don't just be good at it, be the best you can be.

## FRIENDSHIPS, LIKE GARDENS, NEED NURTURING

Without care, gardens won't thrive. We have to "work the soil" and that means putting steady effort into your relationships. Your sweat will provide the water that will make the garden, or friendship, grow.

## IGNORE THOSE WHO TRY TO DISCOURAGE YOU

These individuals offer nothing. Quite often their lives are going nowhere, and that's where they want to take you. Misery loves company. Don't let them drag you down.

## A FRIEND IS SOMEONE WHO KNOWS EVERYTHING BUT LOVES YOU ANYWAY

Not only is this true of friendships but of your parents and grandparents as well. No one is perfect. People who truly love you will always find and remember the best of you.

## DON'T TAKE ONLY WHAT LIFE GIVES YOU; REACH FOR MORE

Don't be a passive recipient, i.e. don't just keep taking. Remember the adage, "Don't just sit there, do something!" It is truly better to give than to receive.

# THE AVERAGE PERSON SHOULD STRIVE TO BE MORE THAN THAT

Average means mediocre or so-so. Is that what you want out of life? When it comes to school grades, a "C" is average; make your life at least a "B," or better yet, an "A."

> "Take care of your body as if you were going to live forever; and take care of your soul as if you were going to die tomorrow."
> **-Saint Augustine**

Sooner or later we're all confronted with illnesses. Keep a positive attitude. Read about the lives of people who have overcome major mental and physical problems. They persisted because of their personal inner strength and faith. Keep a "never say die" attitude. Don't roll over and give up.

> "We may be through with the past, but the past is never through with us."
> **-Magnolia**

Our past <u>can</u> come back to haunt us. If you've led an honest, respectable life, there won't be any skeletons in your closet.

> "It's nice to be important,
> but it's more important to be nice."
> **-Tip O'Neill, former Speaker of the House**

Being nice should be spontaneous and natural, never scripted. If you're nice to everyone you meet, you'll be important in their lives. Be liked for who you are, not what you are.

## NEGATIVE THINKERS NEVER ENJOY THE BENEFITS OF POSITIVE RESULTS

If you think "I can't do it," it probably won't get done. The greatest minds never had defeatist attitudes. Positive attitudes beget positive results.

## DON'T BE AFRAID OF SUCCESS

Sounds strange, doesn't it? Because of insecurity and/or lack of self-esteem, self-doubt enters the picture, and whether they admit it or not, some people worry about being able to handle success and the many pressures that come with it. As the saying goes, "If you can't take the heat, get out of the kitchen" (Harry S. Truman).

## OVERCOME FEAR THROUGH FAITH

Talk to a soldier, a fireman, or a police officer who has faced life or death situations; you can be certain that just about every one of those individuals prayed to God for help and strength. This is faith: the belief that God will be there to see things through.

> "Fame without honor is like a faint meteor, gliding through the sky, shedding only transient light."
> **-Abigail Adams, wife of John Adams**

If you are ever faced with the choice of gaining fame but only at the expense of others, know that you will never enjoy your notoriety. If that's what you want, then you'll be surrounded by similarly misguided individuals.

## THE GRASS <u>ISN'T</u> ALWAYS GREENER ON THE OTHER SIDE

In many ways, this is really about greed: getting or wanting what your neighbor has. However, you'll often find that if you get what you <u>think</u> you wanted, it isn't anywhere near as great as you thought it might be.

## WHEN DOING A FAVOR, DON'T EXPECT ONE IN RETURN

The reward is in the giving and not in the form of dollars, medals, or plaques; the reward is the warmth that you feel afterward, an emotional lift that you alone will experience by giving something to someone with "no strings attached."

## UNDERSTAND THE IMPORTANCE OF ATTITUDE

If you say "I can't," you probably won't. Believing in your ability to reach your goals is one of the most important predictors of success.

## STRIVE FOR BALANCE IN YOUR LIFE

As with any medicine or drug, it's possible to "overdose" on doing anything in excess. How much is too much? Don't sacrifice family, friends, and having fun by being a workaholic. Control your work; don't let it control you.

## MAKING A LIVING IS NOT THE SAME AS MAKING A LIFE

We've all heard the expression, "Get a life," which is true in this case. It's easy to become so consumed with making a living that you don't have a life. Work is hard, but don't become a workaholic.

> "The purpose if life isn't merely to be happy, but to matter, to be productive, and to make a difference."
> **-Leo Rosten**

There is no need to expand on these issues. This statement says a lot about how to shape your life and your personality.

## DOING SOMETHING—ANYTHING— IS BETTER THAN DOING NOTHING

If you find yourself saying "I'm bored," then something's wrong. Remember the saying, "Don't just sit there, do something." If you're sitting, with nothing to do, get up and take a walk—now at least you're doing something.

## KEEP ASKING YOURSELF, WHAT'S REALLY IMPORTANT?

Keep your priorities in order. With the many responsibilities that may come your way, only you can decide what is the most important to you. That's where your greatest energy should go: work, family, church. It is up to you to put them in order.

If you get knocked down, you have two choices; lie there and be defeated or get up and be stronger for the experience.

Some words to an old Frank Sinatra song say, "Pick yourself up, dust yourself off, and start all over again," and this is true of life. The only way to overcome defeat is to battle back. Growth often comes through adversity.

## DON'T BE CONCERNED WITH DYING; BE CONCERNED ABOUT LIVING AN UNFULFILLED LIFE

Another way of saying this is don't fear an ending but rather that it had never begun. When we die, we go before God and give an account of our time on earth. Can we ever justify going empty-handed, i.e. without ever having used the talents given to us?

> "It's never too late to be
> what you might have been."
> **-George Eliot**

The first four words here, "It's never too late" are very meaningful; essentially, this is about not leaving tasks, dreams, or ideas unfulfilled. How many times have you read about a man or a woman who got their college diploma when they were sixty or seventy years old? Don't reach old age and think, "what if" or "if only I had done this or that." No matter how late it seems: DO IT. I am writing this book in my eighty-fifth year.

> "It's nice to be natural, so be naturally nice."
> **-Barbara Bush, as told to her by her father**

He meant: be yourself and don't be fake. Don't put on airs. Above all, don't pretend to be something you are not.

## To All Young Girls, On Respecting Their Bodies

**-From a Dear Abby column**

"When I saw him, I liked him.
When I liked him, I loved him.
When I loved him, I let him.
When I let him, I lost him."

No further comment needed.

"The greatest good you can do for another is not just share your riches, but to reveal to him his own."

**-Benjamin Disraeli**

Make someone feel good about him or herself; offer praise and bring out the best in those around you. In boosting them, you do the same for yourself.

# GOD NEVER GIVES US MORE THAN WE CAN HANDLE

There will be many times when you may doubt this, but here again is where that word "faith" comes in. God knows our strengths and even more so our weaknesses. We all have our crosses to bear, and with each trial, we become stronger. You may not realize it, but God is almost always helping you to carry that cross.

## NOT BEING PERFECT OURSELVES, WE SHOULDN'T EXPECT PERFECTION FROM OTHERS

No one or anything is perfect. Do some reconstructive surgery regarding your faults; correct them and above all, don't repeat them. This is an ongoing process. Be the best person you can be.

Defining Moments
**-Spirella**
"There's no thrill in easy sailing
when the skies are clear and blue,
there's no joy in merely doing things
which any one can do.
But there is some satisfaction
that is mighty sweet to take,
when you reach a destination that
you thought you'd never make."

If something was too easy, it probably wasn't worth the effort.

"You may be disappointed if you fail, but you are doomed if you don't try."
**-Beverly Sills, Opera Star**

Disappointment is normal after failure, but to surrender to failure is something you can't allow to happen. Knock the "t" off of can't and you have CAN.

## HAVING LOVE IN YOUR HOME IS THE FOUNDATION OF YOUR LIFE

"To love is to be loved." Truer words were never spoken. If you've ever known love, then you'll want to pass it on. Something as simple as a hug, a bedtime story, or a good night kiss can fill a bank of memories that will never be forgotten. Why is it that these little acts of love have been with us for hundreds of years, present in virtually every culture? Because they <u>are</u> acts of LOVE. Have you ever thought about a child without a parent or a loved one and how they go to bed each night? Don't ever stop showing your love.

> "One man with courage is a majority."
> **-Thomas Jefferson**

This isn't just about having courage on the battlefield. Courage, or bravery, comes in many forms: defending the poor, the downtrodden, and those who are unable to speak for themselves. Never be afraid to stand up for what's right.

> "Far better it is to dare mighty things, to win glorious triumphs, even though checkered by failure. . . than to rank with those poor spirits who neither enjoy nor suffer much, because they live in a gray twilight that knows not victory or defeat."
>
> **-Theodore Roosevelt**

Simply stated, make your life worthwhile. Roosevelt says to notice glorious triumphs checkered with failures. Our greatest moments often come after setbacks. Don't live a life in that gray twilight of never having tried your best.

> "It's what you learn after you know it all that counts."
>
> **-John Wooden, basketball coach UCLA**

This is a great thought! Basically, this means that we should never stop learning. The quest for knowledge should never end. One of my deepest regrets is that I don't have the time to read more.

> "When you drink the water, remember the spring."
>
> **-Chinese Proverb**

There are so many possible interpretations of this. The spring is the source, which means the beginning. My particular feeling is that my "source" was my parents; I "drank" from the "stream," which was their love, and I was nourished by this.

> "Things turn out best for those who make the best of the way things turn out."
> **-John Wooden**

It's been said, if life gives you lemons, make lemonade; in other words, take and make the best of what life hands you.

> "Never let yesterday take up too much of today."
> **-Will Rogers**

Yesterday is history, gone, over. Don't dwell on it, rather take something good from it and move on. There's too much to do today, and part of that might be to improve on yesterday.

## REPUTATION IS A TREASURED POSSESSION THAT IS OFTEN NOT DISCOVERED UNTIL IT'S LOST

Gossip, lies, and slander can cause the loss of a person's reputation. Don't ever inflict that on someone. If you hear such talk and know it's not true, defend the person being offended. Stamp out the brush fire of gossip before it becomes a full-blown blaze.

## DON'T LOOK FOR WHAT <u>MIGHT</u> MAKE YOU HAPPY IN LIFE; DEAL WITH WHAT WILL PREVENT YOU FROM BEING HAPPY

Happiness is so often equated with wealth, possessions, etc., but it's very true that money can't buy happiness. Happiness is a feeling that comes from doing the right, and often simplest, things for yourself and others. Think small for big results.

## THE MOST TREASURED POSSESSION THAT WE CAN HAVE IS OUR SPOUSE'S HEART

I think of a devoted married couple with a love so true and deep that it's almost as though they've traded hearts. The cliché "I give my heart to you" has true meaning in a loving marriage. When you're around couples (especially older married couples), look for the gleam in their eyes when they look at each other.

"The harder I worked, the luckier I got."
**-Samuel Goldwyn**

Think about this one. This isn't about winning the lottery or hitting it big in the casino: that's luck. Hard work and dedication will always be the reason for your success. There's a difference between making your own luck and being lucky.

> "Every morning I get up and look through the Forbes list of the richest people in America. If I'm not there, I go to work."
> **-Robert Orben**

Even the wealthiest people go to work, which could the reason that they've been successful; they never rest on their laurels and neither should you. The good things in life come from grinding it out every day.

## THERE'S NO RECIPE OR FORMULA FOR A GOOD SENSE OF HUMOR

Be able to laugh, but never at others. Others love it when a person is able to laugh at himself. Our everyday life is full of humor, and it doesn't take much to find it. Get the "juices" flowing with laughter. Be a pleasure to be around.

## DON'T COUNT ON OTHER PEOPLE'S MONEY MAKING YOU RICH

We'd all like to inherit a lot of money but that's a gift and it isn't the result of your endeavors. If making a fortune is your goal, then work for it. America is and always will be the land of opportunity.

## YOU DON'T HAVE TO BE INTERESTING, JUST BE INTERESTED

You don't have to be the focus of attention or the star of the show. Attention will fall on you merely by actively participating and contributing to a conversation rather than trying to dominate it.

> "It's better to be a has-been than a never-was."
> **-C. Northcote Parkinson**

There's nothing wrong with being a has-been; that implies that at least you've accomplished something in your lifetime. Yes, time may pass you by but you did something and that's all that matters. How can some people go through life without ever leaving a mark?

> "A boy does not become a man
> until he loses his father."
> **-Turgenev**

My father was my hero, my friend, and my role model. I still "talk" to him; even though he's not with me physically, he's always by my side. The most difficult part of losing him was the fact that I was never able to hear his voice again. I like to think that I became my father. Nothing could make me happier.

## MANY TIMES, WHAT YOU DON'T DO CAN DETERMINE WHO YOU ARE

This is very meaningful. Strength of character comes from the ability to say no, to take a stand, or to do what your conscience tells you to do. This is about integrity. Don't sell your soul to get ahead.

> "Time heals what reason cannot."
> **-Seneca**

It's been said that time heals all wounds and that's true, but it also hopefully allows for us to look back and evaluate the decisions we've made and how we've lived. Reasoning implies clear, rational thinking, and age gives us the privilege to realize that mistakes we made in our youth were usually from exuberance and not from wrongful intentions.

## IF THERE WERE NO CLOUDS, WE COULDN'T ENJOY THE SUNLIGHT

Dark times in our lives are the clouds, and when we get through them, the sun appears brighter than ever. The "sun" in this case is the good that follows the bad, the positive after the negative. We always appreciate the warmth and glow of the sun after cloudy days.

> "God does not take away trials or carry us over them, but he strengthens us through them."
> **-E.B. Pusey**

It's true that God gives us no more than we can handle. When things seem really difficult, you may have doubts, but know that God knows what He's doing, and who are we to question? No one goes through life without trials. It's how we handle them that matters. Count on God to be your guide and at your side.

> "The deeper that sorrow carves into your being, the more joy you can contain."
> **-Kahlil Gibran**

Throughout my life, there always seems to be a balance between sadness and joy. As much as it hurts to lose loved ones, especially my parents, I take at least an equal amount of joy from the memories they left me and the love of those I cherish the most: my family.

> "Better to light one candle than to curse the darkness."
> **-Chinese Proverb**

This is so simple yet so meaningful. Essentially it means, among many things, to open your eyes, and don't have tunnel vision. Our eyes are the light of our mind and if you go through life with them closed, you see nothing and can do nothing. Take off the blinders.

> "Our main business is not to see what lies dimly at a distance, but to do what lies clearly at hand."
> **-Thomas Carlyle**

Take care of what must be done today: what is at hand. The future can look murky so do your work when and where the light is the brightest, and that's today. The light will shine through into tomorrow—the future.

> "And now these three remain: faith, hope and love. But the greatest of these is love."
> **-1 Corinthians 13:13 (NIV)**

Nothing more needs to be said regarding this beautiful thought.

> "What you have once enjoyed you can never lose. . . All that we love deeply becomes a part of us."
> **-Helen Keller**

A college professor who taught me often said, "Not only do we have a memory, we also have a "forgetory," and it's the latter that helps us to forget the negatives in our lives. Our memory is our safe deposit box filled with pleasant thoughts, events, etc. to which only we have the key.

## THERE'S NO SUCH THING AS THE PERFECT MAN OR WOMAN

Look for the overall package of kindness, ambition, intelligence, and a fun-loving personality. This will be a person who will be easy to love and one who will be capable of giving much love in return.

## GET USED TO THE UNEXPECTED

Life isn't always as organized as we'd like it to be. In my life, just as everything appeared to be falling nicely into place, something would happen and another crisis would arise. Don't ever think you've got it made.

## ONE OF THE FIRST THINGS TO GO STEADY WITH IS A JOB

There are many definitions for the word "steady"—stable, sure, true, level, constant. All of them can apply to a job and how you do it, but also to your life and how you live it. I like the expression "steady as a rock."

# IT'S NEVER TOO LATE TO FIND OUT WHO OR WHAT YOU MIGHT HAVE BEEN

Sometimes it takes a while to find our place in the grand scheme of things. Some people know early on what they can do, while others may never be that lucky. We all have a destiny. Some people are born into it, but most of us to create our own. Don't worry about when it's going to happen, just be certain that you make it happen.

> "Live on the east side of the mountain.
> It's the sunrise side, not the sunset side.
> It is the side to see the day that is coming,
> not to see the day that has gone."
> **-Tom Lea, Artist**

Obviously, this doesn't mean that you physically live on a mountain; it's really about waking up each day with a positive attitude. So many times the word "attitude" has a negative connotation to it; make yours a constant, positive attitude. Wake up each day on the right side of the bed.

## TIME IS AN EXCELLENT HEALER BUT A TERRIBLE BEAUTICIAN

We grow old and the roadmap of our journey appears in the lines on our faces. I love to look at the faces of older people. These are what I call "character" faces. These individuals have nature's facelift; they show the quality of their lives on their faces.

## ONE OF THE LOWEST STATES IN LIFE IS APATHY

Apathy is a moribund state. If it was a creature, it would be a slug or a snail, almost inert, with little motion. Staying active helps to prevent us from becoming apathetic.

> "The truth is that many people set rules to keep from making decisions."
> **-Mike Krzyzewski, Duke University basketball coach**

Rules allow for little or no flexibility. I prefer the term "suggested guidelines" because this allows leeway and with it comes the decision-making process. If you analyze it, you're making hundreds of decisions daily so why get stressed out when the big ones come up? They just take more time and thinking.

> "Nobody has ever measured, not even the poets, how much the heart can hold."
> **-Zelda Fitzgerald**

This is a beautiful thought. How can anyone or any machine measure an emotion as great as love? There is no electrocardiogram or blood test that can reveal the depths of our feelings, and there never will be. Only you will be able to determine these feelings, in your own way.

## DON'T EVER DO ANYTHING TO HURT OR EMBARRASS YOUR PARENTS

Even if your parents aren't alive, ask yourself the question: "Would mom or dad be okay with what I'm considering doing?" You'll always make the right decision using that approach. You have your reputation and their reputation to uphold.

> "If winning isn't everything,
> why do they keep score?"
> **-Vince Lombardi**

The "score" doesn't necessarily pertain to athletic events but rather the game of life. It was mentioned earlier that it would be terrible to look back on your life and end up with a zero in the scorebook... that means that you never even got out of the starting block.

## HOW LOVED AND POPULAR YOU WERE WILL BE DETERMINED BY THE WEATHER ON THE DAY OF YOUR FUNERAL

Sounds a bit pessimistic, doesn't it? A lot of lip service is paid to people throughout their lives, but how people pay their respects to your family will tell the tale. One of the largest funerals I ever saw was that of my father's, a simple, hard-working man who was loved by everyone. I'll never forget the outpouring of love.

# BAD JUDGMENT RARELY RESULTS IN A GOOD OUTCOME

How can good come out of something bad? It can't. Will what I do hurt or embarrass me or my family? If what you're about to do doesn't feel right, then you better re-think the idea.

> "It is the heart always that sees, before the head can see."
> **-Thomas Carlyle**

In this case, the heart creates a "gut" feeling that is rarely wrong. Listen to your heart/gut, and you won't go wrong. So many times, our first impressions are right on the money; call it instinct and go where your heart leads you.

> "No one can take advantage of you without your permission."
> **-Ann Landers**

Be firm. Don't be afraid to say no or to speak up. One of the smallest words in our vocabulary is "no," and so often it's one of the most difficult words to say. Don't be a human doormat by allowing others to take advantage of you. You can be nice and popular, but don't lose your values in the process.

## FOR THE MOST PART, THE WORLD IS RUN BY "C" STUDENTS

Brainpower or a high IQ doesn't necessarily equate with common sense or guarantee success. Is the bottom man in the graduating class of his medical school less of a doctor than the top student? Hard work is the equalizer.

> "We reach for the stars as
> we rush to our graves."
> **-Al McGuire, Marquette basketball coach**

As in a horse race, when we reach the final turn, we realize there's so much to do but so little time in which to do it. This is so true in my case: missions to be accomplished, goals to be met. I'm constantly asking God to grant me "just a little more time."

> "Cowards die many times before
> their deaths; The valiant never
> taste of death but once."
> **-Shakespeare**

I love this quote. This is about the integrity with which we have lived our lives. Valiant means having lived our lives in an upright, honest fashion, without allowing our morals to be compromised. The coward suffers the constant fear (death) of being caught time after time.

> "A journey is a person in itself;
> no two are alike."
> **-John Steinbeck**

Life truly is a journey and the manner in which we choose to live it tells a story—a living novel—that is all truth and no fiction. My journey has been a joy. Will you be able to say the same?

## JOY IS LIKE THANKSGIVING DINNER; PUT DOWN YOUR FORK FOR A MINUTE; YOU MIGHT FIND THAT YOU'RE ALREADY FULL

Joy comes from within, from the heart, from the depths of our souls. Happiness and joy are not the same; happiness is the result or response to an event, and while it is a pleasant feeling, it is not joy which is deep, emotional fulfillment.

# MAKE A CONSCIOUS EFFORT TO KEEP IN TOUCH WITH FAMILY AND FRIENDS

"Around The Corner"
by Charles Hanson Towne

Around the corner I have a friend,
In this great city that has no end,
Yet days go by and weeks rush on,
And before you know it, a year is gone.

And I never see my old friend's face,
For life is a swift and terrible race,
He knows I like him just as well,
As in the days when I rang his bell.

And he rang mine but we were younger then,
And now we are busy, tired men.
Tired of playing a foolish game,
Tired of trying to make a name.

"Tomorrow" I say! "I will call on Jim
Just to show that I'm thinking of him",
But tomorrow comes and tomorrow goes,
And distance between us grows and grows.

Around the corner, yet miles away,
"Here's a telegram sir," "Jim died today."
And that's what we get and deserve in the end.
Around the corner, a vanished friend.

~~~

I've made the mistake of saying I'd call someone "but never got around to it." That happened to me once, and just as in the poem, that friend died. Now I never put off keeping in touch with loved ones.

## PUT THE NEEDS OF OTHERS BEFORE YOUR OWN

Don't be a "me first" kind of person. Be considerate of others' needs and feelings. You elevate yourself by elevating others. Open your ears and heart to those around you.

> "The church is not a hotel for saints,
> it is a hospital for sinners."
> **-Saint Augustine**

We may never become saints, but that doesn't mean we can't go to heaven. Lead a good life, and as the Bible says, "Love your neighbor as you would yourself." Follow the golden rule.

## LET OLD WOUNDS HEAL

Don't hold grudges or stay angry. An untreated wound heals poorly and leaves an ugly scar. If you've been hurt by words or actions, forgive and forget, and the sooner the better.

## DO MORE THAN PUTTING IN A DAY; PUT SOMETHING INTO THE DAY

Be productive. Don't hide from work or try to get by doing as little as possible; that's actually cheating. Remember, "a day's pay for a day's work." (That's what my father always told me.)

## QUIET THE ANGER IN YOUR HEART

There's nothing good or positive about anger. Nothing is ever gained by it. When you're angry, as hard as it may seem, smile, and you'll find that even the worst rage can be subdued; anger will disappear.

## BE A GIVER, ASKING NOTHING IN RETURN, AND LET HAPPINESS BE YOUR REWARD

Giving is truly a reward in and of itself, and the more quietly you give, the better it is and the better you'll feel about yourself. Do it without a lot of fanfare. If you give to be noticed, there is no reward; the thrill is lost.

## ALWAYS GIVE PEOPLE THE RESPECT THEY DESERVE

Below is the code that is recited daily at the Andre Agassi Prep School in Las Vegas, Nevada.

> "The essence of discipline is respect:
> Respect for authority
> Respect for others
> Respect for self
> Respect for the rules"

An attitude of respect begins at home and is then reinforced at school and applied throughout life.

## TODAY IS ALL YOU HAVE; DON'T WASTE IT

We don't get many second chances so don't waste time or opportunities. As you grow older, you'll find that each day becomes more precious than the day before. So why wait until you're older to realize what you've just been told?

## TWO DAYS YOU SHOULD NEVER WORRY ABOUT ARE YESTERDAY AND TOMORROW

Today is what it's all about. We make today better by what we learned or did yesterday. Tomorrow is another day that will be taken care of when it comes. There's no use in rushing it. Make it through today.

## DON'T CLING TO OUTGROWN WAYS; ACCEPT NEW IDEAS

This doesn't mean that the old ways are no longer good; it means that we should keep an open mind and be willing to accept change.

## BE THERE FOR THOSE WHO ARE HURTING

We all have times in our lives when we need someone. The comfort you receive when someone holds your hand or says a few kind words will stay with you, always. Don't shy away from giving comfort to others. During these times, words often don't need to be spoken.

## WISDOM FOLLOWS A LIFE WELL LIVED

If our life has been well lived, it means that we did much, learned much, and collected gems of knowledge and experience. We pass these on to those around us whom we hope have something to gain from our life's experiences.

> "If you think your teacher is tough, wait till you get a boss."
> **-Bill Gates**

Whether you realize it or not, authority figures are getting you ready for real life. Unless you inherit a business or start one up by yourself, you <u>will</u> have a boss. Be a good worker and when the time comes, you'll be a good boss as well.

## IF YOU MESS UP, IT'S NO ONE'S FAULT BUT YOUR OWN

Don't make excuses or point fingers at someone else. If you can take the credit for doing something good, then have the courage to stand up and admit that you messed up.

> "Judge your success by what you have to sacrifice in order to get it."
> **-Dalai Lama XIV**

Success without sacrifice is rare. The harder you work, the greater the pleasure of your rewards. Remember, no one ever drowned in sweat.

## BOTH COOKING AND LIFE SHOULD BE APPROACHED WITH RECKLESS ABANDON

Be spontaneous. Have fun. Don't ever allow yourself to get trapped in boredom. Laugher can be contagious. Choose laughter. Don't bring others down.

# DON'T WASTE TIME

We never know how much time we have remaining. Time wasted can never be retrieved. You can "make up" time, but once lost, it can never be replaced.

> "I believe in angels."
> **-I Have a Dream, a song sung by the Swedish group, Abba**

I truly believe in angels; in fact, I always feel the presence of my parents; they are my guardian angels. They were there for me every day of my life so why should things change now that they're gone?

> "The trouble with being a good sport, is that you have to lose to prove it."
> **-Croft M. Pentz**

This sounds worse than it is; none of us go through life with an undefeated record, but the occasional setback should be a character builder. Just don't get in the habit of losing. Don't ever let yourself get labeled as a "loser."

## YOU CAN'T WIN THE GAME WATCHING FROM THE SIDELINES

Get involved. Just don't stand around. Remember the saying, "don't just stand there, do something." This applies to how you go through life. Instead of wishing that you could be like "other people," be that person. No one can stop you but yourself.

## BE GENTLE WITH THE EARTH

Just as with your room, keep it clean. Don't litter. This is where you live. Keep it clean for those who will follow you.

## TRAVEL

Other than what you learn in school, at home, or from your grandparents, the greatest education comes from seeing the world. Take every opportunity to travel and keep a diary of your adventures so that someday you can reflect on those wonderful times.

## SHARE YOUR KNOWLEDGE

If you have a skill or a talent, pass it on. You can be remembered for what you've done by letting others share your talents. You can create a ripple effect, by passing on what you've learned to others. Think about the beautiful legacy teachers leave to the thousands of students they teach over the years.

## GOD IS THE ONE CONSTANT IN OUR LIVES

God never changes. He's always there. He always listens. He knows what He's doing, and He is the steadying force throughout our lives. Put your trust in His strength.

## TIME CAN'T BE BOTTLED; DON'T WASTE IT

Wouldn't it be nice if we could buy a bottle of time? Maybe a gallon, or more just to be safe, and when we think our time is running out, we would be able to open the bottle and continue on. Sadly, that's not the case so we have to use what's allotted to us as efficiently as we can.

## WHEN YOU'RE IN TROUBLE AND YOUR KNEES START TO KNOCK, TRY KNEELING ON THEM

This is a simple idea, but in some situations, it can be steadying to just kneel and pray. It's difficult to walk on weak, wobbly knees; a kneeling position anchors you and gives you stability. And while you're on your knees, you might even say a little prayer.

## DON'T JUST KEEP THE FAITH, SPREAD IT AROUND

Don't be afraid to show that you're a good Christian. Good Christians have been conspicuous throughout the centuries because of their actions and the way they live: living a life of good examples. A beautiful song is entitled, "They Will Know We Are Christians by Our Love."

## DON'T THINK YOU'RE BETTER THAN OTHERS

This little poem says it so well.

> "Stunned Surprise" (Author Unknown)
> I dreamed death came to me one night,
>   and Heaven's gates flew open wide.

With kindly grace, St. Peter came
and ushered me inside.

There, to my astonishment, were friends
I had known on earth.
Some I had labeled as unfit
and some of little worth.

Indignant words flew to my lips,
words I could not set free.
For every face showed stunned surprise—
No one expected ME!

## IF YOU WANT TO REMAIN YOUTHFUL, REMAIN USEFUL

No matter how old you are or what the status of your health may be, you can always do something. Don't spend your golden years in a rocking chair; there's no forward motion in a rocking chair—no progress—movement, but nothing else.

"I think of life as a good book. The further
you get into it, the more it
begins to make sense."
**-Harold S. Kushner**

Life is like a good book; the more you get into it, the more you understand it and enjoy it. Reading a good book can be a very stimulating and wonderful experience. Life can be the same, but it's up to you to make it so. Approach each day as a new page in the book of your life and make it even more interesting than the previous "page."

## BE PATIENT WITH YOURSELF

So often we tend to be our own worst enemies. Life is tough enough without putting more pressure on yourself. Recognize your weaknesses and work through them; don't let them drag you down.

## NO ONE EVER RESENTS A KIND WORD

The <u>way</u> you say something can be more hurtful than what you say. "Nice" words can be said in a sarcastic manner. Give thought to your words and when your words are spoken kindly they will be well received.

## LISTEN FOR GOD'S ADVICE

This doesn't mean that He's actually going to whisper in your ear. God is always in our hearts, and if we "listen," we never go wrong. God speaks and comes to us in many ways. . . always stay tuned in.

## DON'T BE TOO AFRAID OR TOO PROUD TO ASK FOR HELP

Some of the best education I received came from people who never even went to high school—my grandparents and my parents. They taught all the values that no school could ever offer. I've tried to live my life by how I saw them live theirs. Don't put yourself above others because of what you perceive to be a lack of education.

> "Don't laugh at one who is old, for surely the same will happen to you."
> **-Chinese Proverb**

This is all about respect. Respect the lives the elderly have lived, the wisdom they offer, and their strength that has allowed them to live so long. Love, honor, and respect them.

## WHEN YOU FEEL LOST OR LONELY, GO TO GOD; HE'LL GUIDE YOU HOME

"LOST" here means confused or uncertain. When you don't know which way to turn, turn to Him.

Close your eyes, hold out your hands, and let Him lead you. You'll never get "lost."

## SUCCESS IS OFTEN MEASURED BY WHAT WE DO FOR OTHERS

Most people measure success by monetary achievements, but the true measure of success is how you treated your fellow man. What did you do for others? The fun is in giving. How I envy the philanthropist who has millions to give away and who gives it away anonymously.

## TAKE CARE OF YOURSELF SO THAT YOU MAY TAKE CARE OF OTHERS

Realize that one day you may have to take care of an elderly parent (or two). Be mentally and physically prepared. Love and care for them in their old age as they cared for you when you were an infant.

> "Four things come not back: the spoken word, the sped arrow, the past life, and the neglected opportunity."
> **-Aiki Flinthart**

Again, this tells us to think about our actions: what we do and how what we do can affect others. . . what we say as much as <u>how</u> we say it. Don't look back on a life full of missed opportunities. The past can be beautiful, but if lived poorly, it can come back to haunt you.

## A LIFE WELL SPENT SHOULD BE YOUR GOAL

Really, this isn't much to ask of yourself. A life lived to the fullest, where at the end of each day you were able to say, "I did the very best I could do and nothing less."

> "Children are the living messages we send to a time we will not see."
> **-Neil Postman**

This is about the legacy we leave our children, not a financial one, but a legacy of our traditions, the manner in which we lived our lives, and the sincere hope that our descendants will follow the examples of those before them and continue to pass on that legacy.

> "Of all nature's gifts to the human race, what is sweeter to a man than his children?"
>
> **-Marcus Tullius Cicero**

Every day of my life, I thank God for the blessing of my children. Can there be any greater gift? To my children and grandchildren I say, "If you love and enjoy your family as much as I have, you will know the meaning of true joy."

> "The longer I live, the more I read, the more patiently I think, and the more anxiously I inquire, the less I seem to know. . . Do justly. Love mercy. Walk humbly. This is enough."
>
> **-John Adams, The Letters of John and Abigail Adams**

I love John Adams: a simple man who rose to the greatest levels and a person who felt he could never stop learning. Follow his lead. Read his biography.

## TAKE GOD'S HAND AND WALK WITH HIM

This means to offer yourself and what you do to God each day and put yourself in His hands. Let Him lead the way and you'll never go wrong.

> "The greatest mistake you can make in life is continually fearing that you'll make one."
> **-Elbert Hubbard**

A great leader, President Franklin D. Roosevelt, once said: "We have nothing to fear but fear itself." Fear can paralyze, and that renders you helpless. Look fear in the eye. Don't ever let it control you.

> "You cannot discover new oceans unless you have the courage to lose sight of the shore."
> **-André Gide**

Don't stay anchored at the dock, i.e. with fixed ideas, lifestyles, etc. Yes, security is nice, but don't be afraid to test the waters of new challenges. Think about the early mariners who sailed uncharted waters. What in our lives is as daunting as that?

> "Our greatest glory is not in never falling, but in rising every time we fall."
> **-Confucius**

This is the best summed up by recommending that you see in the movie "RUDY" (1993).

> "Nothing is more difficult, and therefore more precious, than to be able to decide."
>
> **-Napoleon Bonaparte**

This has been addressed before. We make decisions throughout the day, it's this decision-making ability requires the use of our brain, making us unique. The more difficult the decision, the greater the sense of achievement.

> "Nothing in life is to be feared,
> it is only to be understood."
>
> **-Marie Curie**

Here's that word "fear" again. If you can know and understand what your fear is, you've already overcome it. Start by asking yourself, "Why am I afraid of this or that?" Very often fear is no more than self-doubt, or lack of confidence. Don't doubt yourself.

> "Life is a continued struggle to be what we are not, and to do what we cannot."
>
> **-William Hazlitt**

This isn't about overachieving; it's about saying I can do it when others tell you, "You can't." Who are they to put limitations on you? You and only you know what you're capable of doing.

> "If there is no wind, row."
> **-Latin Proverb**

These are six simple words, but they say so much and can be interpreted so many ways. To me, it means don't wait for something or someone to do it for you. You have to take the initiative to get things started and complete them. Use all the resources at your disposal.

> "You've got to get up each morning with determination if you're going to go to bed with satisfaction."
> **-George Horace Lorimer**

The greatest satisfaction comes with the knowledge that "I had a good day: a positive, productive one. I did my best."

## DON'T BE AFRAID TO SAY I LOVE YOU

These words are as powerful as any that have ever been spoken or written, but say them from the heart, otherwise, they're meaningless. Say what you mean and mean what you say. I get a thrill each time my children or grandchildren tell me they love me. I never tire of hearing those three little words.

## DON'T ABANDON OLD-FASHIONED PRINCIPLES. THEY NEVER GO OUT OF STYLE

Love, honor, and respect were the principles my parents instilled in me. They never "lectured" me about these ideals, but I learned by watching them live their lives in quiet dignity.

> "The human mind is not a deepfreeze for storage but a forge for production."
> **-Rabbi Benzion C. Kaganoff**

Yes, we store a lot in our minds, but the mind's primary function is to create. Use the storage area as a place to draw from, and don't worry about running out of storage space.

> "In the middle of every difficulty lies opportunity."
> **-Albert Einstein**

Even the greatest of minds such as Albert Einstein encountered obstacles, but rather than be deterred, he took advantage of a negative situation, turned it around, and made something positive out of it. Difficulties and obstacles are merely bumps in the road.

## AN APOLOGY NEVER DIMINISHES A PERSON; IT ELEVATES THEM

Some might equate apologizing with weakness, but nothing could be farther from the truth. It takes a strong, confident person to offer an apology. Both parties benefit from that act.

## WALK TALL AND SMILE A LOT

A pleasant, smiling person creates a "presence." People love being around happy people. A warm smile can be like a magnet that draws others to you. Know that when you walk into a room, your presence will mean something.

## DON'T BE A MENTAL LOAFER

Read something that requires thought, effort, and concentration. It's okay to read the comics and the sports page (I do every day), but don't stop there; read the rest of the paper and above all, the editorials. Just read.

## MAKE A CONSCIOUS EFFORT TO BE AGREEABLE

This doesn't mean being a "toady" (a yes man) in order to be popular or well-liked. Being pleasant and having a positive attitude, without being condescending or patronizing makes for an agreeable personality.

## DON'T MAKE PROMISES YOU CAN'T KEEP

Think before you make a commitment. Will you be able to follow through on your promise? It might be better to say, "I'll try my best," or "I'll do anything I can to help you." Remember, think with your heart.

## SHOOT FROM THE HIPS AND NOT THE LIPS

Talk is cheap, as the saying goes; having the strength to stand by what you say is what really matters. Loose, glib talk does not have substance—like trying to nail jelly on a wall, it won't hold.

## DON'T JUST SEIZE THE DAY, RUN WITH IT

Enjoy every day, not only in what pleasures it can bring but also in how productive you can make it; it's up to you. Just as with your time, don't waste it. There's only one today.

> "Most people in this world are about as happy as they have made up their minds to be."
> **-Abraham Lincoln**

Just as we can control our destiny to a great extent, we can control our happiness. Wake up happy and in a good mood, with an equally good attitude. Be certain there's no wrong side of the bed to get up on.

## TIME IS ONE OF OUR MOST VALUABLE COMMODITIES

Use it. . . don't waste it. Take advantage of it. Don't take too many timeouts during your lifetime.

> "He who has never learned to obey cannot be a good commander."
> **-Aristotle**

This doesn't take much thought. How can a person expect others to follow him or her if he or she has never been able to listen to other authorities? Some of our greatest leaders have been people who "worked themselves up through the ranks," i.e. they started at the bottom, and along the way learned to lead, by following first.

"It is not the critic who counts; not the man who points out how the strong man stumbles, or where the doer of deeds could have done them better. The credit belongs to the man who is actually in the arena, whose face is marred by dust and sweat; who strives valiantly; who errs, who comes short again and again, because there is no effort without error and shortcoming; but who does actually strive to do the deeds; who knows great enthusiasms, the great devotions, who spends himself in a worthy cause; who at best knows in the end the triumph of high achievement, and who at worst, if he fails, at least he fails while daring greatly so that his place shall never be with those cold and timid souls who know neither victory nor defeat.

**-President Teddy Roosevelt**

Theme: A collection of inspirational and motivational proverbs, quotes, adages etc.

Motivation: The original concept was for these quotes to be used in my memoirs, but as the number grew, it appeared obvious that such a large collection would be best serve as a text.

A special thanks to my granddaughter, Brett, who made this manuscript possible with her time, talent, and energy. Without her, it would not have become a reality.